MW01615404

DACHAU CONCENTRATION CAMP MEMORIAL SITE
A TOUR

DACHAU CONCENTRATION CAMP MEMORIAL SITE
A TOUR

THE HISTORY OF THE DACHAU CONCENTRATION CAMP AND THE DACHAU MEMORIAL SITE

An historical overview

On March 22 1933, the Nazi regime opened a concentration camp on the grounds of the disused Königlich Bayerische Pulver- und Munitionsfabrik Dachau, a defunct factory complex that once produced gunpowder and ammunition. This prison and place of terror existed for twelve years. More than 200,000 prisoners from over 40 nations were imprisoned in the Dachau concentration camp and its subcamps; at least 41,500 persons died here of hunger and illness, from the torture they suffered, were murdered, or perished from the consequences of their imprisonment. After U.S. Army units had liberated the prisoners on April 29 1945, the American military government used the former prisoner camp as a Displaced Persons camp. From July 1945, the grounds served as an internment camp for suspected Nazi perpetrators; in 1948, the Bavarian state government set up a refugee camp. Thanks to the initiative of the survivors, who had joined forces in 1955 to form the Comité International de Dachau (CID), it proved possible to turn the onetime prisoner camp into a place of commemoration and remembrance. The Dachau Concentration Camp Memorial Site, featuring a documentary exhibition, opened in May 1965. To the present day, it is the goal of the Dachau Concentration Camp Memorial Site to remember the suffering and death of the prisoners, and to facilitate and foster analysis and discussion of Nazi crimes. In the following, a chronological survey presents the most important events in the history of the Dachau concentration camp and the various uses of the grounds after 1945.

The grounds of the disused gunpowder and munitions factory, 1933

Detained in an area not under legal jurisdiction: the establishment of the Dachau concentration camp as a prison for political opponents

After the appointment of Adolf Hitler to the position of Reich Chancellor on January 30 1933, the National Socialists, tolerated by their coalition partners, immediately set upon undermining the rule of law and unleashing a wave of terror, needing only a few weeks to achieve their goal of establishing a dictatorship in Germany. The systematic persecution and elimination of political opponents, especially those organized in the labor movement, played a decisive role. Following the Reichstag fire on the night of February 27–28 1933, which the Nazis blamed on the Communists, Reich President Paul von Hindenburg issued the "Reichstag Fire Decree". The regulations of this decree suspended key basic rights and legalized the imposition of "protective custody" as a preventive measure to suppress political resistance. The Gestapo (Geheime Staatspolizei/Secret State Police) – in Bavaria until 1936 the Bavarian Political Police (BPP) – were empowered with immediate effect to incarcerate persons in concentration camps without needing a court order and for an unlimited period. Beginning on March 10 1933, waves of arrests were launched in Bavaria, targeting Communists, Social Democrats, Socialists, trade unionists, and specific members of the conservative Bavarian People's Party.

Under the command of the Nazi Party's paramilitary organizations, the Schutzstaffel (SS) and the Sturmabteilung (SA), acting together with region-

The first prisoner transport at the gatehouse of the former factory grounds, March 22 1933

al civilian authorities, more than 80 concentration camps were opened throughout the Reich in 1933. The goal was to eliminate political opponents and detain them in an area that was not subject to legal jurisdiction. The Nazi leadership was looking for suitable locations to set up "protective custody camps" where they could imprison political opponents on a mass scale. In Bavaria, Heinrich Himmler chose Dachau. Himmler was the head of the SS and appointed commissarial police president of Munich in March 1933. Located close to the town of Dachau was the grounds of a disused gunpowder and ammunition factory. The expansive compound with production buildings and workers' barracks was largely abandoned.

The first convoy of prisoners arrived at the grounds on March 22 1933. The Dachau concentration camp was the first state-run concentration camp in Bavaria and one of the first concentration camps established in the Reich. Unlike smaller camps elsewhere however, the Dachau concentration camp remained in operation until the end of the war and was developed into the model for the Nazi concentration camp system.

On April 11 1933, Heinrich Himmler, meanwhile also Chief of the Bavarian Political Police, handed authority over the Dachau concentration camp to the SS. This signaled the actual beginning of the brutal regime of terror. Himmler installed the SS colonel Theodor Eicke as camp commandant in June 1933. Eicke set about reorganizing the camp and introduced a tightly organized administrative and command structure. He issued a set of "disciplinary and punishment regulations" to be enforced on the prisoners. These regulations ranged from detention for days at a time and "hard labor" through to floggings and execution by shooting. A catalogue of "service regulations" inculcated SS guards to proceed "without tolerance, with the upmost, irreconcilable, disciplined severity" and to be ruthless in their use of firearms. Outwardly, these regulations signalized a set of binding rules for all; in reality however, they hardly did anything to curb the despotic violence the SS inflicted on the prisoners. The life and death of the prisoners lay in the hands of the camp SS.

Another aspect of the "Dachau model" was the indoctrination of the SS men on site at the camp. Located next to the prisoner camp was an extensive garrison area in which the SS leadership and guard troops were drilled ideologically and militarily. Antisemitism, racism, and hate for political opponents were the main foundation of this training. Appointed to the post of chief of the "Concentration Camps Inspectorate" in 1934, Eicke institutionalized and systematized the use of violence against prisoners. The "Dachau model" was installed in all subsequently established concentration camps. This "Dachau school of violence" produced several concentration camp commandants.

Political prisoners in the Dachau concentration camp, SS propaganda photo, May 24 1933

Heinrich Himmler (l.) and Theodor Eicke (r.),
SS propaganda photo, around 1941/42

Roma from the Burgenland,
SS propaganda photo, July 20 1938

The imprisonment of so-called "community aliens"

German political opponents to the Nazi regime formed the largest prisoner
group until 1938. Besides members of the labor movement, conservatives
and representatives of various Christian faiths, in particular members of the
Jehovah's Witness, were the targets of political persecution. Jews were also
imprisoned in the Dachau concentration camp, at this stage for alleged political offenses and not because of their background. Increasingly, more and
more groups who failed to fit the Nazi ideal of the "Volk community" were
exposed to intensified discrimination and persecution. From the fall of 1933,
alongside regime opponents, persons were also imprisoned for "reasons" of
racial ideology and "social hygiene". Sexual and ethnic minorities like homosexuals and Sinti and Roma were regarded as "alien to the community". Persons who had repeatedly committed criminal offences or led a nonconformist
life were stigmatized as "professional criminals" and "asocials", and placed
in concentration camps. The issuing of the directive on "preventive crime
combating by the police" in 1937 systematized this course of action. Following an order from Himmler, meanwhile the Chief of German Police, in 1938
the Criminal Police rounded up thousands of persons without any judicial
warrant and detained them in preventive custody as part of "Operation Work-

Deportation of Jewish citizens from Baden-Baden to the Dachau concentration camp, November 10 1938

Shy Reich". These included persons with previous convictions, prostitutes, beggars, the homeless and unemployed as well as addicts and persons with sexually transmitted diseases. Scores of Sinti and Roma were also imprisoned.

The expansion of the Dachau concentration camp

As part of the preparations for war, the concentration camp system was considerably expanded to serve as an instrument of domestic terror between 1936 and 1939. With the exception of the Dachau concentration camp, all the camps of the early years were abandoned. At the same time, new and far larger concentration camps based on the "Dachau model" were built. It was in this context that in Dachau the prisoner camp was newly built and the SS camp expanded in 1937/38. The SS had the old barracks demolished and forced the prisoners to perform the extremely arduous building work under harsh conditions. Completed within a year, the new prisoner camp was planned to hold 6,000 prisoners.

Between the spring of 1936 and early 1938, prisoner numbers remained roughly between 1,700 and 2,500 persons. After German troops occupied

Austria and the Sudetenland in 1938, thousands of political prisoners, Jews, and Sinti and Roma were first transported to the Dachau concentration camp from the German-occupied territories. The Nazi regime was pursuing a politics of violent expansionism in Europe: it employed "protective custody" as an instrument to eliminate opponents and pacify captured territory.

In May and June 1938, two prisoner transports, each with 600 Jews from Vienna, arrived at the Dachau concentration camp. In the aftermath of the anti-Semitic pogroms of November 1938, around almost 11,000 Jewish men were transported to the camp. The SS extorted and abused them to force them into giving up their assets and to emigrate. At least 190 Jews died in the ensuing months as a direct result of the terror of the camp SS. Most of those sent to the Dachau camp in November 1938 were released. In mid-1939, a few hundred Jews were still being held in the Dachau concentration camp. Jews were the most frequently mistreated prisoners by the SS guards, bullied, abused, and murdered.

At the end of September 1939, the prisoner camp of the Dachau concentration camp was temporarily vacated. The SS required the grounds to train the SS division "Death's Head" and therefore transferred the almost 5,000 prisoners to the concentration camps Buchenwald, Mauthausen, and Flossenbürg. At these camps, their imprisonment and living conditions deteriorated so severely that many of the prisoners died before relocation back to Dachau began in the spring of 1940.

The escalation of SS terror in the Dachau concentration camp during the Second World War

Whereas at first mainly Germans were imprisoned, from 1940 onwards more and more prisoners were sent to the Dachau concentration camp from countries occupied by the German Army. From the ca. 200,000 persons imprisoned in Dachau between 1933 and 1945, some 40,700 came from Poland, more than 32,000 from the German Reich, ca. 25,000 from the Soviet Union, ca. 21,300 from Hungary, ca. 14,100 from France, and ca. 9,600 from Italy. Besides these six largest national prisoner groups, prisoners from numerous other occupied countries were incarcerated in the Dachau concentration camp.

In summer 1940, the number of prisoners rose to ca. 10,000. At the same time, the death rate escalated. In 1939, the registry offices listed 183 deaths in the Dachau concentration camp; a year later, the figure was 1,575. The SS had two crematoria built in the commandant's headquarters area to cremate the bodies and erase all traces of their crimes.

Scores of clergy were imprisoned in the Dachau concentration camp, most of them Polish priests who were arrested as representatives of their country's Catholic elite. From the end of 1940, the Dachau concentration camp functioned as a collection camp for Catholic, Protestant, and Orthodox clergy. Of the 2,729 imprisoned clergy, 1,780 were Polish.

Once the war began, the SS escalated the terror in the concentration camps and living conditions for the prisoners deteriorated dramatically. Working conditions were murderous. Bullying, severe punishments, torture, and other violent excesses were the order of the day. Food, hygienic conditions, and clothing were all fully inadequate. The prisoners were helplessly exposed to the elements, unprotected from the cold, wet, and heat.

The Nazi regime began to use the concentration camps as execution sites. After the attack on the Soviet Union in June 1941, the Gestapo ordered the shooting of Soviet POWs in the Dachau concentration camp. These men were "segregated" after being categorized as Jews, intellectuals, or Communist functionaries in the Red Army. Violating international law, the SS murdered over 4,000 POWs at the SS shooting range Hebertshausen in 1941/42. Political opponents were murdered in the bunker courtyard and the crematorium area.

Beginning in 1941, SS and mental hospital doctors began to murder concentration camp prisoners categorized as unfit for work as part of the Nazi regimes "euthanasia" program. Every concentration camp was set a number that corresponded to around one-fifth of their respective prisoner contingent. In 1942, in so-called "invalid transports", 2,524 prisoners, both ill and those deemed no longer capable of work, were sent from the Dachau concentration camp to Hartheim Castle in Austria. A nursing home for mentally handicapped persons, Hartheim Castle was converted into a killing facility for the "euthanasia" program in 1940. Using poison gas, facility personnel murdered ill and handicapped persons as well as forced laborers and concentration camp prisoners. In the Dachau concentration camp, SS doctors killed ill and disabled prisoners with phenol injections.

From 1942, prisoners were the victims of cruel pseudo medical experiments. These included malaria experiments considered relevant for the planned settlement of the southern regions of the Soviet Union, as well as "biochem-

Prisoners stacking bricks,
SS propaganda photo, July 20 1938

Prisoners working in the SS armory,
SS propaganda photo, around 1942

ical" and sulfonamide experiments to treat infected wounds. In addition, medical experiments serving research on survival chances at high altitudes or distress at sea, commissioned by the German Air Force, were carried out. Hundreds of prisoners died because of these horrific experiments performed by the camp doctors.

The deportation of Jews and Sinti and Roma to the extermination camps

After the invasion of the Soviet Union in June 1941, paramilitary death squads ("Einsatzgruppen") of the Security Police (Sipo), the Security Service of the Reich Leader SS (SD), and other SS and police units murdered more than 500,000 persons in the conquered territories up until 1942. In February 1942, "Operation Reinhardt" was launched, the systematic murder of Polish Jews in the extermination camps of southeastern Poland. Jews from the German Reich and the occupied territories of Europe were deported to the Auschwitz extermination camp from the end of 1942. After the occupation of Hungary in March 1944, the SS deported 430,000 Jews to Auschwitz.

Beginning in 1941, paramilitary death squads of the Sipo and SD, along with units from the Order Police and the German Army, also murdered thousands of Sinti and Roma in occupied Poland, the occupied territories of the Soviet Union, and Serbia. Following orders by Heinrich Himmler, from February 1943 through to the summer of 1944, the SS deported some 22,600 Sinti and Roma from the German Reich and the occupied territories to the extermination camp Auschwitz-Birkenau, 19,300 of whom died.

The development of a system of subcamps for forced labor

In the early years of the Dachau concentration camp, the work imposed on the prisoners often served as harassment and punishment. Jewish prisoners and inmates accused of some offense had to do extremely grueling work in the gravel pit. Beginning in 1938, the work of the prisoners was used for specific building projects of the SS and its expanding economic enterprises. The SS continued however to use exhausting manual labor as an instrument to punish and terrorize the prisoners.

After the so-called "Blitzkrieg strategy" against the Soviet Union failed, the Nazi regime adjusted to the demands of a protracted war. In the spring of 1942, the regime decided to deploy concentration camp prisoners as forced laborers in war production on a large scale. Armaments workshops were set up in the concentration camps, but primarily external work details and subcamps were located near armament manufacturers. The Dachau concentration camp had under its authority a vast network of 140 subcamps, predominantly in southern Bavaria. The prisoners were forced to work mainly in the air armaments sector. The SS "hired out" prisoners to economic enterprises crucial to the war effort in exchange for payment, while the companies profited from the labor of the prisoners. The SS transported the prisoners to the work site and was mostly responsible for guarding, providing rations and living quarters, as well as medical care. For many prisoners, working in factories meant improved imprisonment and living conditions. A deployment at an outdoor site however, particularly in the construction work details, equated to "extermination through work". An enormous number of prisoners died due to the inhuman working conditions and lack of food, as well as assaults by the guard personnel. The actual number of victims is difficult to ascertain because prisoners unable to work were returned to the main Dachau camp, from where they were then sent to the extermination camps to be murdered. The Dachau concentration camp developed into a collection and distribution point that arranged for the necessary replenishment of new work slaves and replaced those prisoners no longer able to endure the murderous conditions.

In 1941/42, the murder and terror in the Dachau concentration camp reached an initial peak. Hunger and disease aggravated the situation further, in particular a typhus epidemic in the winter of 1942/42.

In 1944, with Allied air raids increasingly inflicting damage on and severely hampering armaments production, the Armaments Ministry planned to build bombproof, underground manufacturing sites. The two largest subcamp

Prisoners in front of the bunker construction site at the Landsberg subcamp, around 1945

In the Hurlach subcamp (Landsberg-Kaufering complex) prisoners had to live in earth huts, April 28 1945

In the Ampfing subcamp (Mühldorf complex) the SS quartered the prisoners in primitive fiberboard structures called "Finn tents" in the woodlands, May 7 1945

complexes of the Dachau concentration camp, in Mühldorf and Landsberg-Kaufering, were set up. This undertaking demanded an enormous labor force. In the summer of 1944, Adolf Hitler thus ordered the deportation of Jewish prisoners from the concentration camps at Auschwitz, Kaunas, and Warsaw, as well as from Hungary, occupied by Germany since March 1944, to the Reich. In the subcamps of Mühldorf and Landsberg-Kaufering, a large number of Jewish prisoners were forced to build enormous bunkers that were to house production facilities for fighter planes. More than 30,000 prisoners had to endure murderous imprisonment and working conditions; over one-third of them did not survive the ordeal.

"Evacuation transports" and "death marches" in the final phase of the Dachau concentration camp

Originally built to hold 6,000 persons, the prisoner camp was permanently overcrowded from the summer of 1940 to the end of 1942, with up to 11,000 prisoners incarcerated. The prisoner numbers continued to rise even further however – in the final months before the end of the war, the number of prisoners in the main Dachau camp was far in excess of 30,000. In these months "evacuation transports" from other concentration camps arrived continuously in Dachau. The overcrowding of the camp became dramatic; the hygiene conditions and the supply situation were catastrophic.

From 1944, the impending defeat of the German Armed Forces was becoming increasingly apparent, with the Red Army and the Western Allies advancing relentlessly towards the borders of the German Reich. The SS responded by disbanding all the concentration camps close to the frontline, in the Baltic countries, in occupied Poland, and in Western Europe. In the summer of 1944, the SS began transporting prisoners under disastrous conditions from the abandoned camps to concentration camps within the Reich, including Dachau. Crammed into overcrowded freight wagons, a large number of prisoners died during these transports.

The death rate in the Dachau concentration camp rose dramatically in the final months of the war. Between 1933 and 1945, ca. 41,500 persons lost their lives here; more than one-third died in the final six months. Due to the overcrowding – and because the SS did nothing to alleviate the situation – infectious diseases like typhus and spotted fever spread, causing the death of thousands of prisoners. Towards the end of April 1945, the SS then began to transport prisoners from the Dachau concentration camp to prevent their liberation by Allied troops. On April 26, a goods train with more than 2,000

Prisoners greet their liberators, May 1945

Jewish prisoners left the camp. On the same day, almost 7,000 prisoners, arranged into columns of ca. 1,500 persons, were forced to depart Dachau on "evacuation marches" – which the prisoners themselves called "death marches" – in the direction of Tyrol. Prisoners who from sheer exhaustion collapsed or could not keep up were either shot by SS guards or beaten and left on the side of the road. Several thousands of prisoners failed to survive the "evacuation transports" and the forced marches.

The liberation of the prisoners and the prosecution of the perpetrators

On April 29 1945, two separately arriving units of the U.S. Army – the 45th infantry division Thunderbird and the 42nd infantry division Rainbow – liberated the Dachau concentration camp. Over 32,000 prisoners were in the main camp at the time. Jubilant, they swarmed to meet their liberators. American soldiers liberated the survivors of the "death marches" in southern Bavaria, the last on May 2 1945. On the very same day as liberation, survivors of different nationalities founded an international camp committee. Thou-

Typhus Ward - G.I's Arrive

U.S. soldiers look after former prisoners suffering from typhus, April/May 1945

sands of prisoners lay dead between the barrack blocks and in front of the crematorium. They had to be interred. Up until the end of June 1945, the camp grounds were used as quarters for former prisoners who were ill, had no place to return to, or were waiting to be repatriated. They were supplied with food and medicine by the U.S. troops. For thousands of former prisoners, help came too late however. They died of exhaustion, from diseases, and the consequences of concentration camp imprisonment. The prisoner committee supported the American military government in organizing the running of the camp and functioned as the self-administrative body of the liberated prisoners. There was no return home for most of the Jewish survivors: their family members were murdered, the basis for any kind of livelihood destroyed

In July 1945, the American military government converted the former prisoner camp and the SS camp into an internment camp for suspected Nazi offenders with a capacity to hold 30,000 persons. Members of the Nazi Party and the SS, members of the German Armed Forces, war criminals, and civilians were imprisoned here.

Attracting considerable public interest, the Dachau Trials took place on the grounds of the former SS camp between 1945 and 1948. These trials involved 489 proceedings in front of American military courts. The first trial focused on crimes committed in the Dachau concentration camp. Many of the accused pleaded the need to act under superior orders as a means to avoid admitting individual guilt. They presented themselves as merely subordinates obeying orders – if they had not carried out these orders, so their argument, they would have risked life and limb. In fact, members of the SS on all levels of the hierarchical command chain in the camp had considerable room for maneuver. Many of the offenders were directly involved in the crimes and they not only bullied, abused, and killed prisoners under orders – they also acted on their own initiative. The military courts based their judgements on the Anglo-American legal tradition of "common design". The prosecution had to prove that all of the accused had collectively run and willingly supported the criminal camp system. All of the 40 indicted were found guilty; 36 were of them were sentenced to death, with 28 of these sentences carried out.

This main trial was followed by 121 trials involving around 500 defendants. These trials were also concerned with crimes committed in the Dachau sub-camps and other concentration camps. In 1949, the West German judiciary assumed responsibility for the criminal prosecution of Nazi crimes.

The subsequent use of the grounds – from internment camp to residential estate for expellees

In January 1948, the U.S. authorities handed over a large part of the former prisoner camp to the Bavarian state. Due to the acute lack of living space available after the war, the state government decided to use it to accommodate ca. 2,300 ethnic German expellees from Eastern Europe. The barracks were altered to fit their new purpose and given new interiors. Businesses covering everyday needs opened, so too inns, medical practices, a primary school, a kindergarten, and a post office. Over the years, the reception camp was referred to as the "Residential Estate Dachau East". The last residents left the estate in 1965.

The crematorium area was the only place on the grounds dedicated to commemorating the victims of the Dachau concentration camp in the immediate postwar years. Accessible to the public, the area was cared for as a memorial site. Postwar society in Germany and Dachau generally sought to pass over the crimes committed in the Nazi years and repress the memory of what hap-

Courtroom during the Dachau Trials, December 1945

Children playing in the
"Residential Estate Dachau East", 1963

Visitors in the crematorium area, 1963

19

The former prisoner Adi Maislinger guides visitors through the Dachau Concentration Camp Memorial Site, 1980s

pened. Although the town had close economic, administrative, legal, and personal ties to the concentration camp, the population of Dachau asserted to the U.S. military government that they "knew nothing" about the crimes committed in the camp. The residents claimed that they themselves had been victims of the Nazis and had tried to resist the regime. As everywhere in Germany, this refusal to face up to questions of guilt and responsibility went hand in hand with a relativizing construction of the "other Dachau", a town that had nothing to do with the atrocities perpetrated in its direct vicinity. As a result, interest in the history of the Dachau concentration camp and the fate of those persecuted was limited at first. It was thus left to the survivors organized in the International Dachau Committee to make the decisive contributions on the path to the founding of a memorial site.

The founding of the Dachau Concentration Camp Memorial Site

A supplementary agreement to the Paris Treaties signed in 1954 between West Germany and France placed the gravesites of victims of the Nazi regime under special protection. In 1955, the Comité International de Dachau (CID) was founded in Brussels as the successor organization to the International Camp Committee. The principal goal of the survivors' association was to create a memorial site on the grounds of the former prisoner camp.

In 1956, the CID succeeded in convincing the Bavarian state government of the necessity of a dignified place of remembrance. The Dachau Concentration Camp Memorial Site was then opened on May 9 1965, the twentieth anniversary of the liberation of the concentration camp. From now on, visitors could inspect the building remnants of the concentration camp and a highly-regarded documentary exhibition in the former maintenance building.

It is thanks to the initiative of the CID that an International Monument could be unveiled on the Memorial Site grounds in 1968. In keeping with the political and social conditions in Bavaria, a Christian interpretation of the historical site predominated. In the years before, a Catholic chapel, a convent, a Protestant church, and a Jewish memorial had already been erected on the grounds.

Until 1972, the U.S. Army used the onetime SS camp, the former Jourhaus, and the western wing of the former maintenance building as a garrison headquarters. The former detention building served as a prison for military personnel. In 1972, the Bavarian Riot Police took over the area once covered by the SS camp.

The presence and engagement of survivors strongly shaped the work at the Dachau Memorial Site in the years immediately after its opening. At first, only a few youth groups and school classes visited the Memorial Site. From the mid-1970s onwards, the Dachau Memorial Site developed more and more into a place of historical and civic education. "Forgotten" victim groups like Sinti and Roma, homosexuals, and Jehovah's Witnesses made their voices heard in the 1980s. Visitor numbers from Germany and abroad rose steadily. Soon, school classes made up the majority of visitors.

Since the 1980s, history associations formed by engaged Dachau citizens have actively campaigned for and fostered commemorative work in their town. As public interest in the fate of the victims and the work of the Memo-

The survivors Bogdan Dębowski, Jerzy Wojciewski, and Andrzej Korczak-Branecki (left to right) from Poland commemorate the dead on the 65th anniversary of liberation, May 2 2010

rial Site increased, in particular with the fiftieth anniversary of liberation in 1995, the negative attitude of the town authority to the Memorial Site began to change gradually, and it is meanwhile a key player in historical work on site. After decades of effort by civic initiatives and fierce controversies amongst local interest groups, in the spring of 1998 the Jugendgästehaus Dachau, an international meeting place under the trusteeship of the Free State of Bavaria, the City of Dachau, and Dachau District, was finally opened.

Redevelopment work on the Dachau Memorial Site began in 1997. A new main exhibition was opened in 2003. The leitmotif of the exhibition, still to be seen today, is the "Path of the Prisoners". It documents the fate of those persecuted, from their arrival at the camp, their life, suffering, and dying here, through to liberation. The historical education revolves around presenting biographies of prisoners and using an array of literary and artistic contemporary testimonies from prisoners, as well as the historical sites themselves. Since May 2005, visitors can enter the grounds via the historical path through the Jourhaus, the entrance gate to the onetime prisoner camp. This enables visitors to gain a better overall understanding of the topography of the earlier concentration camp.

The survivor Dr. h.c. Max Mannheimer at a contemporary witness talk in the Visitors' Center, February 7 2013

In 2003, the Bavarian state government handed over responsibility for both the Dachau and Flossenbürg Concentration Camp Memorial Sites to a new foundation, the Stiftung Bayerische Gedenkstätten. The task of the foundation is to maintain and foster the Memorial Sites as places of international learning and remembrance for future generations.

Today, up to a million people from around the world visit the Dachau Concentration Camp Memorial Site annually. The former prisoners still alive are meanwhile elderly. The current challenge facing the Memorial Site and its work is to keep alive knowledge about Nazi crimes and foster historical awareness of their importance – even if it is becoming less and less possible to hear firsthand accounts of the fate of the prisoners.

Aerial shot of the Dachau concentration camp, April 20 1945

A TOPOGRAPHICAL LOCALIZATION
BACK THEN ...

This aerial photograph shows the Dachau concentration camp on April 20 1945. The color markings highlight sections of the concentration camp, each of which fulfilled different functions.

The green area covers the prisoner camp. The 34 symmetrically arranged barracks are clearly visible. Prisoners were quartered in 30 of them.

The orange area marks agricultural land the SS euphemistically called the "herb garden". The area was part of the "Deutsche Versuchsanstalt für Ernährung und Verpflegung GmbH" (DVA), an institute established by the SS for the purpose of cultivating and researching medicinal plants. From 1938 onwards, prisoners carried out forced labor here. Due to the brutal working conditions enforced to cultivate the land, the prisoners named it the "plantation".

The area of the commandant's headquarters of the camp SS is marked blue. Located here were the offices of the camp commandant, the quarters of the SS men assigned to guard the prisoners, as well as the crematorium area.

The yellow area is the SS training camp. Here SS men were indoctrinated ideologically and drilled militarily. Also located in this area were administrative, residential, and various storage buildings as well as workshops in which concentration camp prisoners were forced to work. Towards the end of the war, the grounds of the Dachau concentration camp covered more than two square kilometers.

This aerial photograph shows the grounds of the former Dachau concentration camp in 2006. The area of the Dachau Concentration Camp Memorial Site is marked green. The Memorial Site covers the area of the former prisoner camp, the crematorium grounds, and other smaller sections of the former commandant's headquarters. Also located in the latter and marked purple is the Carmelite Convent.

On a large part of the former concentration camp, once the grounds of the SS, are buildings and facilities of the Bavarian Riot Police. The marked yellow area is separated from the Memorial Site by a fence and not accessible to the public. After the war, the American military government used the former SS area as an internment camp and garrison base. In 1972, the Bavarian state government took over the area and based a division of the Bavarian Riot Police there.

The grounds of the former SS experimental agriculture facility / "herb garden" is today largely overbuilt with commercial and industrial firms, but the main ensemble of buildings remains. Today it is owned by the City of Dachau.

Aerial shot of the Dachau Concentration Camp Memorial Site, September 13 2006

HISTORICAL LOCATION AND MEMORIAL SITE

As a comparison of the two aerial photographs from 1945 and 2006 shows, the Memorial Site does not exactly cover the geographical expanse and structural makeup of the concentration camp. After the war, a diverse variety of reuses reshaped and changed the grounds and its building structures. Numerous historical structures were modified, demolished, or destroyed. In some cases only traces and relicts remain.

The development of the grounds into the Dachau Concentration Memorial Site, opened in 1965, followed the principles advocated by the involved survivors, to renovate and preserve the historical building substance considered especially relevant and significant for representing the suffering of the prisoners. Other building remnants were deliberately removed.

Today, the physical remains of the camp's grounds serve as the starting point for presenting the historical repercussions of the politics of persecution and extermination pursued by the Nazi regime. The methodological guideline for developing and arranging the grounds is to secure the relicts and mark them as such. Subsequent reshaping and changing is identified and marked as an added historical layer.

As a place of learning and critical discussion about the history of National Socialism, the Memorial Site has the character of a museum. Exhibitions in the historical buildings meet this task, while in outdoor areas information panels provide orientation for visitors.

Numerous monuments, memorial stones, commemorative plaques, and gravesites are also located on the grounds. As a place of remembrance for the victims of the Nazi regime, the Memorial Site has a particularly important and significant role to play in international commemorative culture.

STATIONS ON THE GROUNDS OF THE DACHAU CONCENTRATION CAMP MEMORIAL SITE
AN OVERVIEW

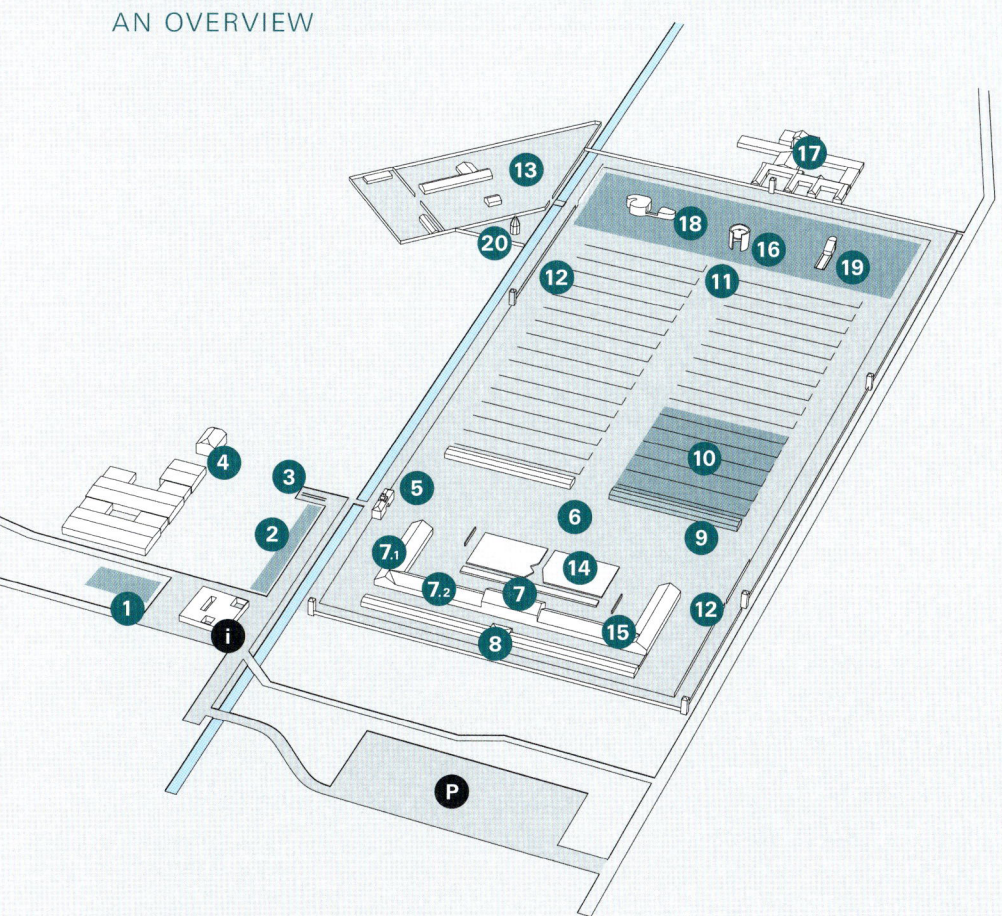

RELICTS

1 Main SS guardhouse
2 Political department
3 Remnants of the first camp and the connecting road to the SS area
4 SS camp
5 Jourhaus with camp gate
6 Roll call area
7 Maintenance building (main exhibition)
   7.1 Shunt room
   7.2 Prisoner baths
8 Camp prison (exhibition)
9 Barracks (exhibition)
10 Sickbay area
11 Functional buildings area
12 Guard installations
13 Crematorium area

PLACES OF REMEMBRANCE

14 International Monument
15 Memorial room (main exhibition)
16 Mortal Agony of Christ Chapel
17 Carmelite Convent
18 Protestant Church of Reconciliation
19 Jewish memorial
20 Russian Orthodox chapel

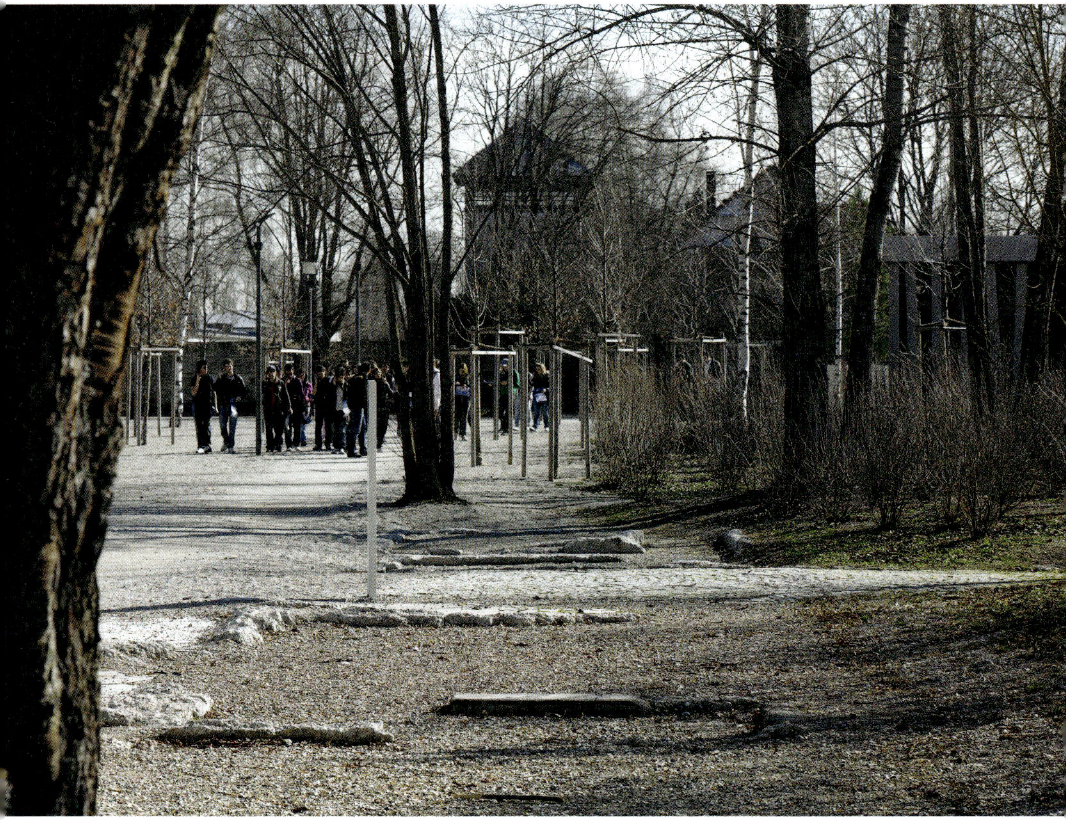

Relicts of the foundations of the main SS guardhouse in front of the Visitors' Center, 2010

The staff car of Heinrich Himmler passes through the gate of the main SS guardhouse, met by a guard of honor of SS men, January 20 1941

Main SS guardhouse, SS propaganda photo, around 1939

1 Main SS guardhouse

Located to the west of the Visitors' Center are the remnants of the foundations of the main SS guardhouse. From 1936, the gate building formed the main entrance to the commandant's headquarters on the SS grounds. This is where the camp SS, responsible for guarding the prisoners, was quartered.

The main SS guardhouse was the place where the arriving prisoners first entered the concentration camp. After arriving at the Dachau railway station, the prisoners were forced to march to the camp under the watch of the SS guards. Buses and trucks were also used to bring the inmates to the camp. Prisoner transports reached the SS camp via the train track that led directly from Dachau station.

Police file photo of Benno Oppenheimer, taken by the political department in the Dachau concentration camp, 1937

2 Political department

Along the path leading from the Visitors' Center to the Jourhaus, eight angle irons mark the onetime position of a historical building: the elongated structure where the offices of the political department of the Secret State Police (Gestapo) were located.

The traumatic registration procedure for the newly arrived prisoners usually began in the rooms of this building. The political department recorded personal information, took police photographs, compiled prisoner files, and assigned numbers to the prisoners. For every prisoner they registered the date of admission, transfer to another camp, release, or death. The political department also interrogated prisoners, often using torture.

Former location of the political department, marked by iron angles, 2017

Embankment wall made of demolition material and the relicts of a section of rail track on the left side of the former connecting road to the SS camp, in the background is the former camp bakery, 2017

3 Remnants of the first camp (1933–1937) and the connecting road to the SS area

In front of the entrance to the former prisoner camp, the Jourhaus, is the connecting road to the former SS camp. To the left and right are sections of an embankment wall that is made of materials from demolished buildings.

The SS used the existing structures of the gunpowder and munitions factory in the earlier camp as the prisoner kitchen, mess hall, and admission room for prisoners (wall to the left), as well as workshops for carpentry, metalworking, and tailoring operations (wall to the right). In the later expanded camp, SS-owned companies were located in these buildings, for instance the SS Clothing Works and the German Equipment Works.

View of the connecting road between
the prisoner camp and the SS camp,
on the left the section of rail track,
May 1945

Aerial shot with a view of a section of the former SS grounds, 1950s

1 Main SS guardhouse (1936–1945)
2 Camp bakery (1933–1945),
  Main SS guardhouse and SS mess hall
  and kitchen (1933–1935)
3 Kitchen and dining hall
  (1933–1937/38),
  later: SS Clothing Works

4 Political department
5 Commandant's headquarters
  (1933–1945)
6 Jourhaus (1936–1945)
7 Carpentry, metalwork, and tailoring
  operations (1933–1938),
  later: German Equipment Works

The structures were torn down in the 1980s. A continuous wall, separating
the Memorial Site grounds from those of the Bavarian Riot Police, was built
out of the rubble. During modification work to the Memorial Site in 2004,
this wall was broken through and the former connecting road uncovered.
In the course of this work, remnants of a section of rail track emerged. This
track was used to deliver materials to the SS businesses in which prisoners
performed forced labor. This section of track was not used for prisoner transports. Located in the factory halls visible today was the camp bakery. Until
1935, the main SS guardhouse as well as the SS mess hall and kitchen were
also housed there.

The commandant's headquarters of the Dachau concentration camp, March 1933

Prisoners pull a roller to surface the road in front of the camp bakery, SS propaganda photo, May 27 1933

The SS guard unit of the Dachau concentration camp, SS propaganda photo, 1933

Robert Ley, head of the "German Labor Front" (c.), during an inspection tour of the Dachau concentration camp, SS propaganda photo, February 11 1936

4 SS camp

The earlier SS grounds, which made up the largest section of the Dachau concentration camp, are not accessible to the public. The Bavarian Riot Police use this area. The demolishing of sections of the embankment wall allows visitors to view important sections of the topography of the former concentration camp.

A section of the former commandant's headquarters, once located directly adjacent to the prisoner camp, can be seen. Still standing today are the former camp bakery (left) and the commandant's headquarters (right). From this office, the commandant issued orders for the guard troops and presided over the main administrative and organizational unit of the concentration camp, the headquarters staff. These leadership ranks were mainly responsible for the crimes committed in the concentration camp. Also located in the

View of the former camp bakery (l.) and former commandant's headquarters (r.), 2017

area of the commandant's headquarters were the living quarters of the armed SS men who manned the towers and kept guard over the prisoner work details, so too, from 1940, the crematorium grounds.

The SS training camp was behind the commandant's headquarters. Stationed here were SS units sent to Dachau for basic and advanced military and ideological training. The Nazi regime developed the SS into an elite organization and military strike force. The grounds were home to a diverse array of facilities for instruction and indoctrination, residential and administrative buildings, as well as maintenance and provision operations. Concentration camp prisoners were forced to work on the building sites and in the various company workshops located in the SS camp.

The Jourhaus with the gate to the prisoner camp, 2010

5 Jourhaus with camp gate

The Jourhaus was the entrance and exit of the prisoner camp, which the SS officially called the "protective custody camp". Located in the Jourhaus were the duty rooms of the camp SS and the staff of the political department. Prisoners were forced to construct the building in 1936 as part of the rebuilding of the camp. "Jourhaus" is a military term. "Jour" is French for "day". Hence, the Jourhaus was where the officer of the day and his staff were stationed. From here, they organized the prisoner work details, controlled the barracks, wrote applications for imposing punishments, and arranged the guarding of the prisoners. From the perspective of their prisoners, the Jourhaus was the center of SS power.

Installed and controlled by the SS, and hence dependent on them, the "prisoner functionaries" assumed a series of guard, supervisory, and administra-

The Jourhaus shortly after liberation with former prisoners and U.S. soldiers, May 1945

"In the gateway a wrought-iron trellis was opened. [...]
The barracks shimmered green through the barbed wire.
Even from faraway one could see that everything was kept scrupulously
clean and not even the smallest scrap of paper lay on the ground.
But something grim, something awful, something ice cold hung over
everything. Never before in my life have I felt a setting to be so
unconditionally dangerous and hostile."

Contemporary witness account of arriving in front of the Jourhaus at the Dachau concentration camp; Edgar Kupfer-Koberwitz, prisoner in the Dachau concentration camp 1940–1945

tive tasks. These prisoners were forced to carry out the orders issued by the SS, even if these orders threatened the health or life of their fellow prisoners – otherwise they could expect to be punished. Many of them used their position to protect their fellow prisoners. Deploying prisoner functionaries was an instrument of SS control.

Every newly arrived prisoner passed through the wrought-iron gate of the Jourhaus with the inscription "Arbeit macht frei" ("Work sets you free"). This saying reflected how the Nazi propaganda aimed to downplay what took place in the concentration camp, presenting it as a "work and education camp". It also revealed the cynical debasing attitude towards the prisoners, for forced labor was one of the main instruments of extermination and terror used by the SS.

Depiction of a nighttime roll call; an ink drawing by the survivor
Karl Freund, finished on December 17 1939

6 Roll call area

The roll call area was located between the maintenance building and the barracks complex. The SS carried out the roll call and the punishments on this vast open space. The prisoners had to assemble in front of the barracks for the morning headcount. From there they marched to the roll call area, where they had to stand at attention in rows of ten. The SS forced the prisoners to remain stockstill in this position no matter what the weather was like. Following roll call, which usually lasted an hour, but frequently took much longer, the prisoners had to line up in their work details. This whole procedure was repeated in the evening after work. If the number of persons counted and reported did not match the official figure, then all the prisoners had to remain standing at attention until the reason for the diverging numbers was found. Only then did the SS allow the prisoners to return to barracks. Ill and frail prisoners often collapsed from exhaustion during roll call. The other prisoners were not permitted to go to their aid. Another collective punishment was drill exercises on the roll call area. The SS forced the prisoners to do physical exercises in the disciplined order of a military drill until they were completely exhausted. Prisoners were also flogged openly in front of their fellow inmates on the roll call area, a punishment that humiliated the victim and intimidated those forced to look on.

The Dachau concentration camp was filled to overflowing in the final months of the war. The continually arriving prisoners from the evacuated concentration camps were first assembled on the roll call area. Many of the ill and exhausted prisoners died on the spot.

The former roll call area, with the former maintenance building on the right, 2017

"For more than three hours we stood on the roll call area and waited for the whistle that was to signal our return to the barracks. A fine rain, cold and penetrating, transformed our wet things into heavy rags. One saw the drops dance in the yellow light of the searchlights over the rigid mass of prisoners, around which the eternally cursing SS men circled like fierce dogs."

Contemporary witness account of standing at attention on the roll call area;
Edmond Michelet, prisoner in the Dachau concentration camp 1943 – 1945

The former maintenance building, in front the International Monument, 2017

7 Maintenance building (main exhibition)

Today, the main exhibition of the Dachau Concentration Camp Memorial Site is located in the former maintenance building. The exhibition presents the history of the Dachau concentration camp and the fate of the prisoners. Also in the building are the memorial room, the special exhibition room, administration offices, as well as the archive and library.

The SS had the structure built as part of the expansion of the prisoner camp in 1937/38. The maintenance building contained various workshops, storage and functional rooms. There the SS deployed the prisoners as metalworkers, electricians, painters, and installers. Inmates had to work in the laundry and the prisoner kitchen. While the kitchen was fitted with modern appliances, provisions were chronically insufficient and the prisoners suffered great hunger. In the maintenance building the SS continued the humiliating procedure for the newly arrived prisoners. The prisoners were registered in the so-called

Maintenance building with the quote from Heinrich Himmler on the roof, SS propaganda photo, around 1939/41

Prisoners carry pails of soup from the kitchen to the barracks,
SS propaganda photo, June 28 1938

Steamers and soup pails in the prisoner kitchen,
SS propaganda photo, June 28 1938

"shunt room". There they had to hand over their clothes and personal items. After having all their body hair shaven, the prisoners were disinfected and showered. They received prisoner uniforms that rarely fitted. The SS administration kept the prisoners' possessions in the effects storeroom, located in the attic of the building.

On the side of the maintenance building roof that faced the roll call area and the barracks, a quote from Heinrich Himmler in large white letters could be read from 1939 onwards: "There is one path to freedom. Its milestones are: obedience, honesty, cleanliness, sobriety, diligence, orderliness, self-sacrifice, truthfulness, love of the fatherland." Given their desperate situation, this saying openly mocked the prisoners. Hardly any prisoners were released from the concentration camp once the war began.

Main exhibition in the former shunt room, 2017

7.1 Shunt room

After arriving in the prisoner camp, the inmates were first taken by the SS to the shunt room in the maintenance building. "Shunt" is a term from the penal system and means a "prisoner transport". The new arrivals were subjected to a degrading procedure, forced to endure the violent deprivation of their personal rights and liberties.

A row of tables was set up between the pillars in the shunt room, dividing the room in the middle. Standing behind the tables were prisoners who the SS forced to work in the so-called "prisoner possession administration". The SS ordered the newly arrived prisoners to strip naked and hand over their clothes and personal possessions. The prisoners at the desks listed these items. The new arrivals then had to move on to the prisoner baths close by, fully naked.

Jurij Piskunov, Ukraine,
undated, prisoner in the
Dachau concentration camp
1943–1945

Stanisław Krzystolik,
Poland, 1930s,
prisoner in the Dachau
concentration camp
1940–1942

Wilhelm Heckmann,
German Reich, 1936,
prisoner in the Dachau
concentration camp
1937–1939

*"We'd stopped being a person. Everything focused on killing off
your sense of shame, breaking your will, and forcing the prisoner into
pitiful blind obedience. It wasn't about if one was an intellectually
or morally valuable human being, everyone was equal and everyone
was judged to be criminal."*

Contemporary witness account of the humiliating arrival procedure;
Hans Carls, prisoner in the Dachau concentration camp 1942–1945

The layout of the exhibition room today takes up the spatial arrangement of
the historical shunt room. Today, display cases are located where the desks
once were, containing original personal items of former prisoners. The sign
"Rauchen verboten" ("Smoking prohibited") on the wall of the former shunt
room was uncovered in 2000.

Richard Blümel (second from the left) with his family, Czechoslovakia, 1930, prisoner in the Dachau concentration camp 1941

Johann Eckstein (second from the right) with his family, German Reich, 1939, prisoner in the Dachau concentration camp 1942

Giovanni Cipollaro (on the right) with his family, Italy, 1938, prisoner in the Dachau concentration camp 1944

The private photos of the inmates reflect their different social backgrounds and personal circumstances. With their arrest and transportation to a concentration camp, they were forcibly cut off from their private, family, and working lives.

Main exhibition in the former prisoner baths, 2017

7.2 Prisoner baths

In the prisoner baths, the new arrivals had their heads and bodies shaven, were disinfected and showered. The SS imposed this procedure not only for reasons of hygiene – it was also designed to deprive the prisoners of a sphere of intimacy and humiliate them. Prisoners were then brought to the baths to shower once a week at first, later less frequently.

After showering, the newly arrived prisoners, harassed by the SS, hastily received a prisoner uniform that in most cases was ill fitting. From 1938 onwards, the uniform comprised a jacket, a pair of pants, and a cap of blue-and-white striped drill fabric. The shoes were made of wood and in part linen. The inmates had to sew their prisoner number and a triangular patch onto their uniform. As of 1938, the SS used these variously colored triangular patches of cloth to divide the prisoners into categories. The classification into prisoner groups was based on the 'reason' for imprisonment given by the Gestapo or the Criminal Police. The triangular patches were symbols of terror in the concentration camps, used by the SS to stigmatize the prisoners and subject them to a hierarchy that meant the chances of survival varied greatly. The SS used the categories intentionally to sow discord amongst the different prisoner groups.

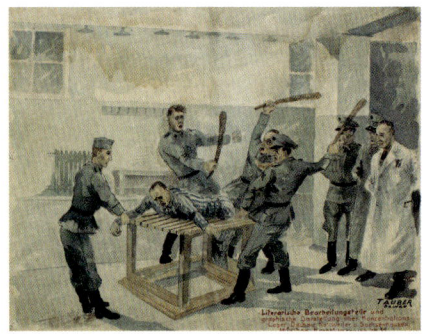

The carrying out of corporeal punishment on the trestle in the prisoner baths, watercolor by the survivor Georg Tauber, 1945

Prisoners were tortured in the baths with "pole hanging", watercolor by the survivor Albert Kerner, 1945

A red patch was used to categorize political prisoners. Jewish prisoners were issued a color patch in addition to a yellow one, so that the two sewn together formed a Star of David. So-called "professional criminals" were forced to wear a green patch. Returned German emigrants were issued a blue patch. Members of the Jehovah's Witness – called the "Bible students" – were marked with the purple triangle. The SS stigmatized the so-called "asocials" with a black patch.

In the prisoner baths the SS punished the prisoners for "violations" of the camp regulations. Bound to a trestle, the prisoners were subjected to vicious beatings. In 1941/42, the SS introduced the torture of "pole hanging".

The former prisoner baths remains unchanged today in terms of its basic layout. The original tub was uncovered during work on the new exhibition, whereas the wooden lattice planks are a reconstruction. The fittings of the beams attached to the pillars, used for the "pole hanging", were discovered while compiling a report on the historical building substance. The main object is a replica of the trestle used for floggings from 1945, which served as evidence at the Dachau Trials.

Liberated prisoners in the baths, April / May 1945

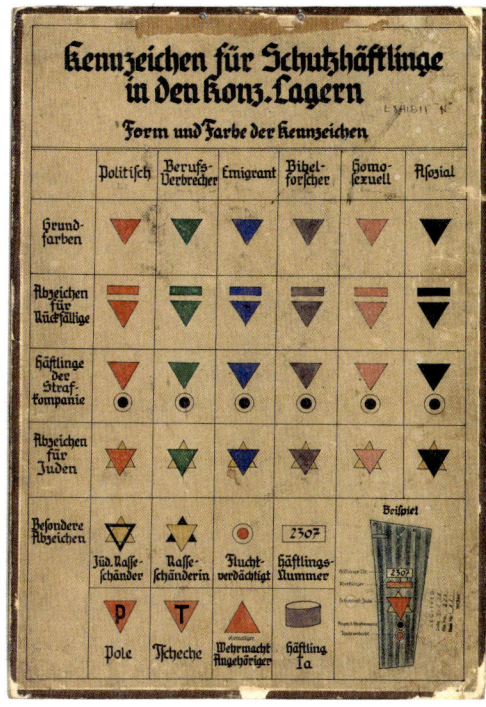

Panel showing the prisoner categories, around 1940

View of the former "bunker courtyard" and the "bunker" (on the right), 2017

8 Camp prison (exhibition)

Located in the former camp prison is an exhibition devoted to the history of the building. For the prisoners, the detention building was one of the main sites of terror, the SS carrying out harsher punishments here. The SS named the building the "garrison detention"; the prisoners called it the "bunker". The prison facility visible today was built in 1937/38.

Located in the square central section were the offices of the guard personnel as well as an examination and an admission room. The interrogation room was insulated to prevent screams from being heard. The SS recorded the personal details of the prisoners and questioned them. In the east and west wings were single cells where the prisoners were locked away under constant surveillance for weeks and months with a minimal supply of rations. The SS mishandled and tortured the prisoners in the camp prison, extracting confessions. Many prisoners died. In 1944, the SS installed four tiny standing cells in the "bunker", measuring a mere 80 cm x 80 cm. The prisoners had to

View of the western "bunker courtyard". The wall is visible in the middle that divided the yard into two sections, May 1945

Depiction of the standing cells, woodcut by the survivor Bogdan Borčić, 1959

"Four months bunker, four months confinement in the dark, four months of getting something warm to eat only every fourth day. Time crawls. I count only every fourth day and am astonished when the food comes and wakes me up. Because I'm in a trance."

Contemporary witness account on solitary confinement in a darkened cell of the camp prison; Erwin Gostner, prisoner in the Dachau concentration camp 1938–1939

endure several days in these extremely cramped, bricked cells, with insufficient air to breathe properly and meagre food rations. From 1941, so-called "special prisoners" were also transferred to the detention cells of the camp prison. These prisoners were prominent public figures the SS kept as hostages, looking to gain some tactical advantage for the war. In 1941/42, a punishment compound for SS men, police officers, and air defense personnel was set up in the east wing of the prison and an annex structure. The latter no longer exists.

The SS used the courtyard between the maintenance building and the camp prison to abuse and murder prisoners. Separated by a wall, the SS set up a shooting stand with stakes and a bullet catcher in the eastern "bunker courtyard". At the end of August 1941, the SS began to execute Soviet POWs there. For reasons of secrecy, these mass executions were then moved to the close-by "SS shooting range Hebertshausen".

Former prisoners in bunk beds immediately after their liberation, May 1945

Prisoners on the camp road between the rows of barracks, SS propaganda photo, June 28 1938

9 Barracks (exhibition)

As part of the expansions made to the camp in 1937/38, the SS had a complex of 34 barracks built. Comprised of four functional and 30 accommodation barracks, the complex was then demolished in 1964/65. The two structures today located where the former camp road began are replicas erected in 1965. The reconstructed barrack on the eastern side features an exhibition on the accommodation and living conditions of the prisoners. Concrete foundations cast in 1965 mark the positions of the other 32 barracks.

Each of the prisoner barracks, also known as "block" in the language of the camp, was divided into four "rooms". Each of these "rooms" was in turn made up of day quarters furnished with tables, stools, and lockers, as well as sleeping quarters with wooden bunk beds. The prisoners were defenseless against the brutal despotism of the SS block leaders who bullied them with strict and minute regulations on the cleanliness of the floors, how things were to be arranged in the lockers, or how the beds were to be made. Even the slightest of deviations from the draconian standards was severely punished.

Each of the accommodation barracks was designed to hold 200 persons; towards the end of the war, the barracks were full to overflowing however, with up to 2,000 prisoners crammed into a barrack. Located in the first barrack on the left of the camp road were the canteen, the camp orderly room, the library, and the SS museum, as well as instruction rooms for the prisoner personnel. On the right of the camp road was the sickbay, which was continually extended to include more barracks given the disastrous state of the prisoners' health. Behind the sickbay were the punishment blocks and quarantine barracks for the newly arrived prisoners.

View of the former camp road and the reconstructed barracks, 2017

"Make the beds! Oh, what a dreadful order, mirroring the whole bloody stupidity of camp discipline. A straw sack is naturally round. But it has to have corners! Like a cigar box. [...]
Planks and little boards surface out of hiding places, specially carved for this purpose. Through a slit in the sack the straw is bulked up with a stick and stuffed against the edge, then a little board is held against it to press it flat. The sheet is carefully spanned over it and a sharp edge is ironed in on the side."

Contemporary witness account of "camp discipline" in the barracks;
Jean Bernard, prisoner in the Dachau concentration camp 1941–1942

View of the former location of the sickbay, 2017

10 Sickbay

The sickbay functioned as a kind of camp hospital and was initially located in the first two functional barracks on the right of the camp road. These barracks were modern and very well equipped. The SS used the sickbay for propaganda purposes: it served as a showpiece for visiting delegations. The sickbay had two surgeries, a medical dispensary, a laboratory, various casualty clinics, and a morgue. In reality however, the ill prisoners had to endure disastrous conditions. The SS doctors generally neglected them. There was, moreover, a blatant shortage of medicine and bandaging materials. It was not until 1943 that prisoners who themselves were doctors were first allowed to care for their ill comrades.

The living conditions of the prisoners worsened rapidly once the war began. Due to malnourishment, lack of hygiene facilities, and physical exhaustion, they were in a terrible state of health. The sickbay was therefore gradually

"The sickbays of the concentration camps, and without fail that of Dachau, had nothing to do with what one imagined [...] hospitals to be. It was an inhospitable place that had no helpful medical atmosphere [...]. Underneath the sham of the surface view was a complete indifference towards the most primitive rules of hygiene and asepsis, and betrayed precisely the state of mind of the SS doctors, who had the task of caring for the inferior cattle which we were."

Contemporary witness account on the sickbay;
Edmond Michelet, prisoner in the Dachau concentration camp 1943–1945

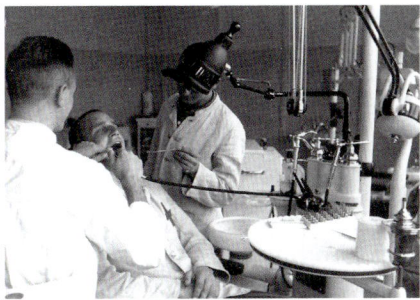

A prisoner is treated in the dental surgery of the sickbay, SS propaganda photo, around 1938/41

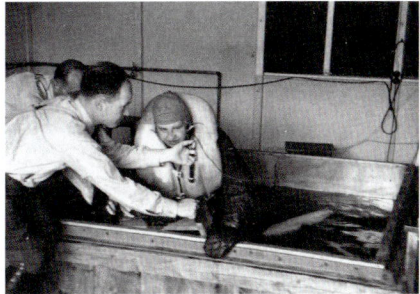

SS doctor Sigmund Rascher (center) during a hypothermia experiment, photographic documentation filed by the SS, 1941

extended to five barracks. It comprised seven "sick quarter blocks" which were connected to one another through a roofed-over passageway. Because of the rapid spreading of infectious diseases, particularly towards the end of the war, the sickbay became a place of mass dying.

Beginning in 1941, SS doctors carried out horrific medical experiments on prisoners there. Commissioned by the German Air Force, they oversaw experiments on the impact of exposure, altitude, and seawater. Prisoners were subjected to life-threatening hypothermic conditions in a water basin, exposed to extreme pressure fluctuations in an altitude chamber, and forced to drink chemically-treated saltwater. Others were infected with malaria pathogens and phlegmon to test medical drugs. Hundreds died during these inhuman experiments.

Aerial shot of the functional buildings in the northern end of the camp, May 1945

11 Functional buildings

Behind the accommodation barracks was a fenced-off area with functional buildings and production facilities where prisoner details were deployed to perform forced labor. The complex was demolished bit by bit in the 1950s and 1960s. Religious sites of remembrance are now located there.

Behind the western row of barracks was the camp nursery (area in red). Saplings and seedlings were grown in the greenhouses that were then later planted in the SS experimental agricultural facility/"herb garden".

Adjacent to the eastern row of barracks, stalls for Angora rabbits were built in 1940 (purple). The breeding station was constantly expanded; by 1944, more than 4,000 animals were being kept there. The wool and fur of the rabbits was used as lining for the uniforms of the German Air Force.

A prisoner at the stalls feeding the Angora rabbits, SS propaganda photo, around 1940/41

A prisoner on the roof of a greenhouse in the camp nursery, secretly taken photo, 1944

On the left, behind the fence, the bordello barrack; on the right, behind the horse cart, the disinfection barrack, May 1945

Disinfection barrack, 1941

In 1941, a disinfection barrack was added (orange) where inmates disinfected prisoner clothing and blankets. Because the SS avoided the building in fear of becoming infected, the prisoners used it to hold secret meetings. They also hid a radio receiver there, enabling them to listen to international broadcasters.

In the spring of 1944, the SS opened a camp bordello (green). Designated a "special building", here women prisoners from the Ravensbrück concentration camp were forced into prostitution. Using a bonus coupon issued by the SS for their rate of work, prisoners could request to visit the bordello. A large majority of the prisoners boycotted the bordello. The SS closed it at the end of 1944.

View of the western guard installation with tower, May 3 1945

Guard installation in the south, behind the former camp prison, 1945

12 Guard installations

Part of the extension work on the camp in 1937/38 included guard installations designed to make escape from the prisoner camp impossible. As the grounds were turned into a refugee camp in 1948, the camp fence and one guard tower were removed. In the 1960s, with the developing of the area into the Memorial Site, the missing guard tower was reconstructed, while the remaining towers, in part in a state of dilapidation, were restored. Sections of the camp fencing were rebuilt to provide visitors with an idea of what the guard installations were like. These reconstructed sections are located to the east of the former maintenance building and at the entrance to the crematorium area.

The prisoner camp was surrounded in the north, east, and south by a three meter-high perimeter wall fitted with barbed wire. In the west, the River Würm served as a natural boundary between the prisoner camp and the SS com-

Reconstructed guard installation in front of the entrance to the crematorium area, 2017

pound. Located on the campside of the perimeter wall and the Würm was an electrified barbed-wire fence, a barbed-wire obstacle, a two meter-deep ditch, and a grass area. The SS cynically called this strip the "neutral zone". If a prisoner entered this area, he was considered to be trying to escape and was shot without warning by the guards. The guard installations included seven guard towers, fitted with machineguns and manned by SS sentries around the clock.

In their absolute desperation, those prisoners no longer able to endure living in constant fear under the SS regime of terror chose to die – they deliberately entered the "neutral zone" or threw themselves against the high-voltage barbed-wire fence. Sometimes the SS guards forced prisoners onto the prohibited area and then shot them because they were allegedly "trying to escape".

New crematorium with gas chamber, called "barrack X", built in 1942/43, 2017

13 Crematorium area

The crematorium area is the main place of remembrance in the Memorial Site. The area was already being used to remember the dead immediately upon liberation. In the 1960s, it underwent a cemetery-like redevelopment. Today, access to the crematorium area is via a bridge from the former prisoner camp. This does not correspond to the historical situation; the area, partly covered by trees, was in fact located in the SS camp, was bounded by a wall, and strictly separated from the prisoner camp. Only SS men responsible for running the facility and prisoners forced to cremate the bodies were allowed to enter.

At first, the SS sent the ashes of the prisoners who perished in the camp to the family concerned, buried the body not far from the camp, or took it to Munich's East Cemetery for cremation. As the prisoner numbers and the death rate rose dramatically with the outbreak of war, in the summer of 1940 the SS had a first crematorium fitted with a furnace built. Just a year later, the capacity of this crematorium was insufficient. In the spring of 1942, work began on building "barrack X", which was then put into operation a year later. This was a crematorium with four furnaces, a disinfection chamber for clothing, dayrooms and sanitary facilities, as well as morgues and a gas chamber disguised as a "shower bath". There can be no doubt that

"Barrack X" in use, secretly taken photo, summer 1944

SS men hang prisoners in the crematorium, watercolor by the survivor Georg Tauber, 1945

"The crematorium can hardly cope with the heaps of corpses laden stark naked like logs on carts, which resemble dung carts, and driven through the gate to be thrown to the embers without a prayer and chiming bells. Even the barbarians were not guilty of displaying such disrespect to the dead."

Contemporary witness account of the conditions prevailing in "barrack X" in January 1945; Karl Adolf Gross, prisoner in the Dachau concentration camp 1940–1945

"barrack X" was designed for the mass extermination of prisoners. Killing people on a mass scale through poison gas never took place in the Dachau concentration camp. It remains unexplained as to why the SS never used the operational gas chamber for this purpose. According to one contemporary witness account, some prisoners were killed by poison gas in 1944. Somewhat secluded from the rest of the camp complex, the SS used the crematorium area as an execution site. Here prisoners were hung or shot in the back of the neck. The victims were mainly members of resistance organizations. A commemorative "path of death" takes visitors past the execution sites and the graves with the ashes. Between 1933 and 1945, around 41,500 persons died of hunger, exhaustion, and disease, or were brutally murdered in the Dachau concentration camp and its subcamps.

STATIONS ON THE GROUNDS OF THE
DACHAU CONCENTRATION CAMP MEMORIAL SITE
PLACES OF REMEMBRANCE

Relief with the triangles linked together in the form of a chain, 2017

Survivor associations attend the laying of the foundation stone for an international monument, September 9 1956

14 International Monument

The International Monument was inaugurated on September 8 1968. It was designed by Nandor Glid, who himself was persecuted as a Jew by the Nazis in his home country of Yugoslavia and had joined the resistance to the German occupation forces at the end of 1944. The sculptor won a competition organized by the CID, the association representing the survivors, in 1959.

The International Monument can be walked through and is made up of different elements. It is based on the idea of a path of education and catharsis. Coming from the Jourhaus, visitors to the Memorial Site face an entry wall. Its inscription calls the visitors to follow the example of the prisoners and actively defend a society without terror and tyranny. The path leads to the lowest point of the Monument, representing the despair and suffering of the prisoners. The central bronze sculpture shows human figures entangled in barbed wire. It is framed by stylized concrete pillars, which symbolize the guard installations.

The International Monument in front of the former maintenance building, 2017

Opposite the sculpture, a relief in the form of a chain symbolizes the solidarity between the prisoners in the concentration camp. The relief features triangles in different colors, recalling how the SS categorized the prisoners. The black triangle for the so-called "asocials", the green triangle for the so-called "professional criminals, and the pink triangle for homosexuals are not represented. These victim groups were not recognized as persons persecuted by the Nazis at the time the Monument was erected. Their fate has only first gradually attracted public interest since the 1980s.

At the end of the ascending path, a tomb contains the ashes of an unknown prisoner. Inscribed into the wall behind the tomb in five languages is the exhortation "Never Again".

Memorial plaque for Cséri Lajos, prisoner in the Dachau concentration camp 1944–1945, donated 2016

The "pink triangle memorial stone" for homosexuals, donated 1985

15 Memorial room (main exhibition)

Currently more than 130 commemorative plaques and stones are in the memorial room at the end of the main exhibition. The room serves to remember individuals and groups imprisoned in the Dachau concentration camp. Private persons and institutions are able to donate plaques commemorating victims of the Dachau concentration camp.

In 2011, three terminals were installed in the memorial room that allow visitors to view the "Book of Remembrance for the Dead of the Dachau Concentration Camp" in digital and printed versions. The remembrance book gives the prisoners who died from the torture inflicted, the inhuman living conditions, or were murdered, their names again, enabling individual commemoration in dignity. Visitors can use the terminals to research the name, nationality, profession, place and date of birth as well as the date of death of the prisoners. The remembrance book contains the names of 33,205 dead. It has proven impossible to identify the names of 8,300 men and women killed in the Dachau concentration camp.

Terminals enable visitors access to the "Book of Remembrance for the Dead of the Dachau Concentration Camp", 2017

View of the memorial room, 2017

Mortal Agony of Christ Chapel and memorial bell, 2017

Consecration of the Mortal Agony of Christ Chapel, August 5 1960

16 Mortal Agony of Christ Chapel

The Catholic Mortal Agony of Christ Chapel was the first religious memorial erected at the northern end of the former camp grounds. The functional buildings of the concentration camp located here were demolished in the 1950s and 1960s.

The Dachau survivor and later auxiliary bishop of Munich, Johannes Neuhäusler, initiated the building of the Mortal Agony of Christ Chapel. The chapel was consecrated on August 5 1960 during the Eucharistic World Congress. Designed by the architect Josef Wiedemann, the open cylindrical structure faces the central axis of the former camp. Above the entrance is a crown of thorns made of copper. Symbolically, the structure stands for the liberation from captivity through Christ. The memorial bell in front of the chapel rings out once a day shortly before 3 p.m., the hour of Jesus's death as depicted in the Bible.

On August 20 1962, the Dachau survivor and later archbishop of Szczecin-Kamień, Kazimierz Majdański, unveiled a bronze likeness of Christ and a trilingual dedication honoring the Polish prisoners, the largest prisoner group in the Dachau concentration camp.

Carmelite nuns building the convent, 1963   Entrance to the Carmelite Convent, 2017

17 Carmelite Convent

Beyond the northern wall of the Memorial Site, behind the Mortal Agony of Christ Chapel, is the Carmelite Convent of the Precious Blood. The order of the Discalced Carmelites was founded by Saint Teresa of Ávila in the sixteenth century. The Carmelite nun Sister Maria Theresia deliberately chose the former Dachau concentration camp because of the horrors that took place here – it was to become a place of offering and prayer, and so establish a living symbol of hope.

The convent was consecrated on November 22 1964 by Johannes Neuhäusler. Josef Wiedemann designed the plan, which takes the form of a cross. The courtyard, the gate, and the church of the convent are publicly accessible through an aperture in a former guard tower. The final resting place of Johannes Neuhäusler is located in the church. In the convent's courtyard, liturgical objects from the camp chapel are exhibited in a vitrine.

Protestant Church of Reconciliation, 2010

The architect Helmut Striffler hands over the key to the Protestant Church of Reconciliation to Bishop Kurt Scharf (center), vice chairman of the Council of Evangelical Churches in Germany, April 30 1967

18 Protestant Church of Reconciliation

The initiative to build a Protestant church came from Dutch survivors, supported by the World Council of Churches. The Evangelical Church in Germany built the Protestant Church of Reconciliation, consecrated on April 30 1967 by the regional bishop of Bavaria, Hermann Dietzfelbinger. The dedication service was led by the retired church president and former Dachau prisoner, Martin Niemöller.

The architect Helmut Striffler designed the building with the church and meeting room to represent a counterpoint to the symmetrical, angular structures and layout of the former concentration camp.

Jewish memorial, 2017

Rabbi David Spiro (center) recites prayers
for the dead at the consecration
of the Jewish memorial, May 7 1967

19 Jewish memorial

On May 7 1967, the regional association of the Israelite Communities in Bavaria unveiled a Jewish memorial. Designed by Zvi Guttmann, the parabola-
shaped structure features a ramp that leads downward, reminding visitors of
the extermination of European Jews. At its lowest point, light shines into the
memorial through an opening.

A menorah – a seven-branched candelabrum – made of marble from Peki'in
is positioned on the top of the structure. The town of Peki'in in Israel symbolizes the continuity of Jewish life.

Russian Orthodox chapel, 2017

Russian soldiers building
the Russian Orthodox chapel,
June 1994

20 Russian Orthodox chapel

Upon the end of the Cold War, public attention began to turn to the fate of
Soviet prisoners, the third largest victim group of the Dachau concentration
camp. The initiative to erect the memorial chapel "Resurrection of Our Lord"
came from the leaderships of the Russian Orthodox Church in Germany and
Russia together with the embassy of the Russian Federation. The architect
Valentin Utkin created the design.

The octagonal wooden structure was prebuilt in Moscow and erected in Dachau by soldiers of the Russian Armed Forces in 1994. The metropolitan of
Nizhny Novgorod and Arzamas, Nicolai Kutepov, dedicated the chapel on
April 29 1995. It sits on a mound, partly comprised of earth from the repub-
lics of the former Soviet Union.

STATIONS NEAR THE
DACHAU CONCENTRATION CAMP MEMORIAL SITE
AN OVERVIEW

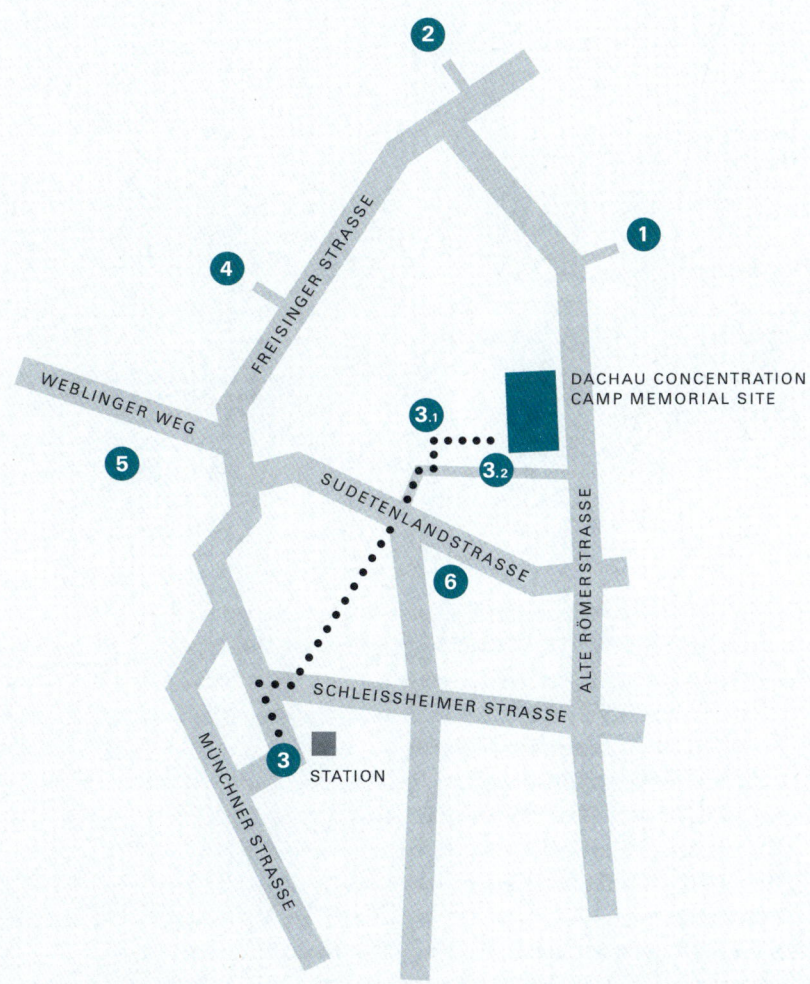

RELICTS

1 SS experimental agricultural facility/
  "herb garden"
2 SS shooting range Hebertshausen
  (outdoor exibition)
3 Path of Remembrance
  3.1 Line section leading to the SS camp
  3.2 SS residential estate

PLACES OF REMEMBRANCE

4 Concentration Camp Memorial
  Cemetery Leitenberg
5 Concentration camp graves
  at the woodlands cemetery
6 Death march monument

The shop (l.) and greenhouses in the "herb garden", SS propaganda photo, 1941

The shot prisoner Abraham Borenstein on the grounds of the "herb garden", SS documentation of the "suicides" of prisoners, May 15 1941

1 SS experimental agricultural facility/"herb garden"/"plantation"

Located outside the prisoner camp was a large nursery with areas of cultivated land that, from 1938 onwards, the prisoners were forced to lay out and work on. The SS described this agricultural operation euphemistically as the "herb garden". Today, the area is mostly overbuilt with industrial buildings.

The complex comprised numerous structures, including a maintenance building, a teaching and research institute, a shop, an equipment shed, a bee house, greenhouses, as well as large sections of productive land. It was Heinrich Himmler's idea that by cultivating and studying medicinal and aromatic herbs the Nazi state could itself independent of its reliance on foreign medicines and herbs. Establishing a "Volk medicine" in close touch with nature was a prestige project of Nazi health policy and was avidly supported by the leader of the SS. Responsible for selling the produce from the experiments and testing was the SS-owned company "Deutsche Versuchsanstalt für Ernährung und Verpflegung GmbH" (DVA).

Former administration and institute building, 2017

The residents of Dachau and neighboring areas could purchase the produce of the "herb garden" in a shop. There individual prisoners succeeded in secretly establishing contact with the civilian population who helped them, at the risk of death, to smuggle goods and information in and out of the camp. The prisoners called the feared deployment to the outdoor areas of the "herb garden" the "plantation" work detail. They were forced to do the extremely arduous and exhausting work no matter the weather. Inadequate clothing, malnutrition, bullying and abuse by the SS turned the already hard outdoor work into a perilous torture. The working conditions in the buildings and greenhouses were less brutal. A work detail of illustrators had to compile a herbarium. The former administrative and institute building as well as remnants of three greenhouses with added end structures have survived. There are plans to restore the building ensemble, which is in the possession of the City of Dachau authority. Based on a new utilization concept, the historical structures are to be integrated into the Memorial Site and become part of its 'space of memory'.

In the foreground the installation "Memorial for the Victims" (2014); behind it the commemorative monument for the murdered Soviet POWs (1964), located in front of the former machinegun and pistol shooting stands, 2017

2 SS shooting range Hebertshausen (outdoor exhibition)

Around two kilometers to the north of the Dachau concentration camp, in the municipality of Hebertshausen, the SS constructed a shooting range in 1937/38. SS units and other military organizations received weapons training there. The facility had five shooting lanes, two shooting stands, a grenade-throwing stand, and a maintenance building. The SS began using it as an execution site in 1941.

On June 22 1941, the war of extermination against the Soviet Union began with the invasion by the German Army. Captured Red Army soldiers were sent to POW camps located in the territory of the German Reich. Together with the German Army, the Gestapo "segregated" 33,000 POWs based on racist and ideological criteria. In violation of international law, Communist functionaries, intellectuals, and Jews were transported to concentration camps and murdered by the SS.

Entrance gate to the SS shooting range Hebertshausen, April 30 1945

Firing practice in the right lane of the machinegun and pistol stand, 1938

Maintenance building with the apartment of the facility attendant, accommodation quarters, offices, munitions store, and inn, SS propaganda photo, around 1942/43

At the Dachau concentration camp, Soviet POWs were mostly killed directly after arriving. The first executions by firing squad took place in the bunker courtyard. Between October 1941 and summer 1942, the camp SS murdered in mass executions over 4,000 POWs at the Hebertshausen shooting range. The SS forced the soldiers to undress and line up in rows of five in the right-hand lane in front of the bullet catcher. Forcibly moved to the left lane, they were then chained to stakes with handcuffs and shot.

After the mass murder of Soviet POWs stopped, the SS then used the shooting range to carry out death sentences passed by the SS and Police Courts.

In 1964, the Lagergemeinschaft Dachau, an association of former prisoners, had the first memorial commemorating the murdered Soviet POWs erected on the onetime grounds of the SS shooting range. In 2014, the grounds were turned into a memorial site with an outdoor exhibition.

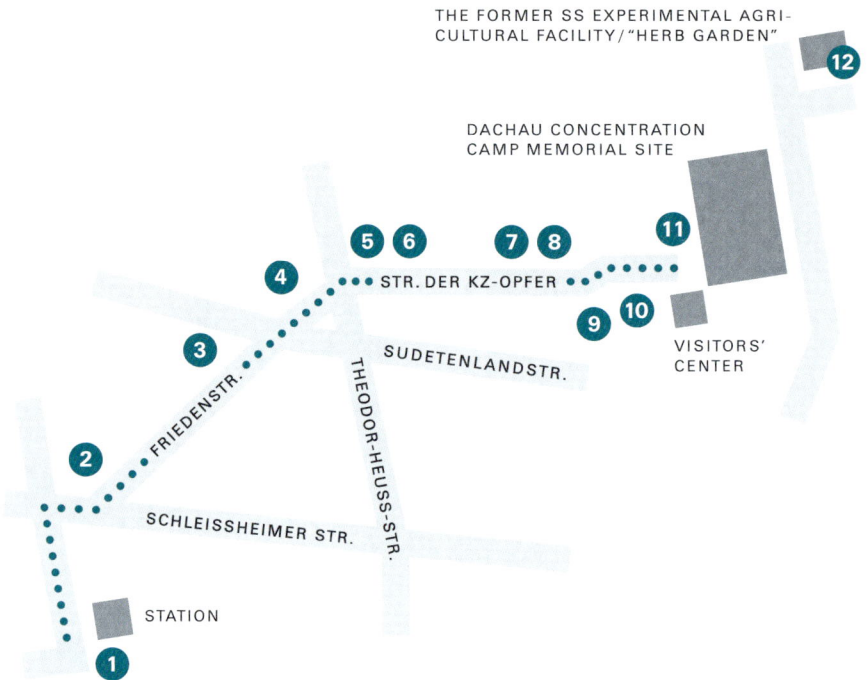

THE FORMER SS EXPERIMENTAL AGRI-
CULTURAL FACILITY/"HERB GARDEN"

12

DACHAU CONCENTRATION
CAMP MEMORIAL SITE

5 6   7 8   11

4   ••• STR. DER KZ-OPFER •••

9   10

3

VISITORS'
CENTER

FRIEDENSTR.

SUDETENLANDSTR.

THEODOR-HEUSS-STR.

2

SCHLEISSHEIMER STR.

STATION

1

3 Path of Remembrance

Inaugurated in 2007, the "Path of Remembrance" is made up of twelve sta-
tions with information panels. The route leads from Dachau railway station
to the Visitors' Center of the Dachau Memorial Site. The walk along the three
kilometer-long path takes around 45 minutes.

The information panels follow the route by which the majority of prisoners
reached the concentration camp, on foot, in trains, or on trucks. The panels
describe the diverse links the town of Dachau had with the concentration
camp and the personal connections of its residents. The railway station served as a "collecting point" for prisoner transports. Dachau's residents could
see how prisoners and, frequently, dead bodies were unloaded from the
trains, and how the SS marched the prisoners to the camp in broad daylight.
Moreover, Dachau residents saw the haggard prisoners who, from 1941 onwards, came to town under SS guard to perform forced labor for local businesses. Also featured on the path are various traces of the past and remnants of building structures. The "Path of Remembrance" ends at the former
SS experimental agricultural facility/"herb garden".

The "death train" from the Buchenwald concentration camp on the section of line leading to the SS camp, April 30 1945

On the "Path of Remembrance": a section of the rail line at Isar-Amperwerke-Straße with panel no. 4, 2017

3.1 Line section leading to the SS camp

A sidetrack led from Dachau railway station to the SS camp. The SS some-times transported prisoners to the site of their imprisonment in goods trains. The newly arrived prisoners passed through the western entrance of the SS camp and on to the barracks area. The sidetrack was removed in 1948. At the former entrance to the SS grounds, where today the Isar-Amperwerke-Straße runs, a small section of the line has survived. Panel 4 of the "Path of Remembrance" marks this location. Two days before the liberation of the Dachau concentration camp on April 29 1945, a prisoner transport from the Buchenwald concentration camp arrived. Loaded with 4,480 prisoners, the train had been on route for 21 days. The SS had crammed the prisoners in goods wagons and given them practically nothing to eat or drink. During the journey, thousands died of hunger and exhaustion or were shot by the SS. A train full of dying and already dead persons arrived in Dachau. Only 816 persons survived the transport. The SS refused the train entry into the SS camp, so that it remained standing on the track in front of the gates. Upon reaching the Dachau concentration camp, U.S. Army troops found the bod-ies in the wagons, a discovery that traumatized many of them.

Office buildings of the Bavarian Riot Police, formerly used as villas by members of the SS, the "Path of Remembrance", panel no. 7, 2017

3.2 SS residential estate

Located to the south of the SS camp were houses and villas lived in by members of the Dachau SS and their families. The residential estate was publicly accessible.

A row of SS villas lined the former "Straße der SS", today called the "Straße der KZ-Opfer". They were built during the First World War and belonged to the gunpowder and munitions factory. Still standing today, they were used by the U.S. Army after liberation. Currently they are home to the offices of the Bavarian Riot Police. Panel 7 of the "Path of Remembrance" provides information on the history of the buildings.

"Theodor-Eicke Platz", named after the second camp commandant, ran along today's "Pater-Roth-Straße". Built by prisoners, the complex comprised, along with residential houses, a bakery, a shop, an inn, a post office, and a "community house" with rooms for holding functions. Today the area is built over with new residential houses.

Residential houses on the "Straße der SS", postcard, undated

Residential complex on "Theodor-Eicke-Platz", postcard, 1941

The corpses of prisoners are transported to the Leitenberg by horse and cart, May 1945

Finding corpses on the Leitenberg, 1949

4 Concentration Camp Memorial Cemetery Leitenberg

Due to a shortage of coal, the crematorium of the Dachau concentration camp ceased operations in February 1945. Between February and April 1945, the SS forced the prisoners to transport the dead bodies to the nearly Leitenberg and dig mass graves for over 4,000 of their fellow inmates.

After liberation, the American military government ordered that two further mass graves be created for some 2,000 dead persons. Former leading members of the Nazi Party and farmers from Dachau had to transport the dead found in the camp by horse and cart to the Leitenberg and bury them there.

The authorities ignored the graves in the immediate postwar years, until the summer 1949, when their uncared-for state triggered an international scandal. The press and politicians demanded that the Bavarian state government create a dignified final resting place for the concentration camp victims.

Cross in the Memorial Cemetery Leitenberg, erected in 1949, 2017

The grounds were redeveloped in line with Christian ideas, without consideration of the various religious beliefs of the victims. The cemetery was consecrated on December 16 1949; a remembrance hall was built in 1951/52.

In the 1950s, the French tracing service conducted exhumations and the dead identified as French citizens were transferred to their homeland. Along with victims from abandoned concentration camp cemeteries in Upper Bavaria, the rest of the dead were reburied on the Leitenberg in single graves. In the 1960s, remains of victims were transferred to Belgium, the Netherlands, Italy, and Norway. The Italian memorial chapel, "Regina Pacis", was consecrated in 1963. Today, over 7,400 victims of the Nazi regime are buried on the Leitenberg.

Terraced graves and mortuary chapel at the woodlands cemetery, 2017

5 Concentration camp graves at the woodlands cemetery

In the northern part of the Dachau woodlands cemetery is a terrace-shaped gravesite that was created for 1,312 concentration camp victims. These persons were former Dachau prisoners who died in the months after their liberation on April 29 1945 from the consequences of their imprisonment.

Between 1955 and 1958, the Italian, French, Belgian, and Dutch tracing services had victims buried at the woodlands cemetery exhumed and transferred to their native countries. In the now unoccupied graves, victims from the "death marches" were reinterred from abandoned concentration camp cemeteries in Upper Bavaria. These victims had initially been buried at cemeteries along the route of the respective march. Buried in the upper row of graves are a few Polish nationals who had worked for the American military government as guards in the Dachau internment camp.

Rows of wooden crosses on the gravesite
for concentration camp victims at
the woodlands cemetery, around 1945

Inauguration of the Jewish memorial at
the woodlands cemetery by Rabbi Max
Grünewald, May 1 1964

Located around the graves are memorials dedicated to Jewish, Polish, and
Austrian victims of Nazi persecution as well as a memorial stone commemorating those who died during the "Dachau uprising" of April 28 1945.

An armed resistance group made up of escaped concentration camp prisoners and Dachau citizens had stormed the town hall, hoping to liberate the
town from the Nazi regime before Allied troops arrived. Units of the Waffen-
SS quelled the uprising and killed six of the resistance fighters. Another memorial plaque on Dachau town hall square remembers the victims of the
"Dachau uprising".

Death march monument at the intersection of Theodor-Heuss-Straße / Sudetenlandstraße, Dachau, 2017

6 Death march monument

With the advance of the Allied troops, from the summer of 1944 the SS began to abandon the concentration camps. The prisoners were transferred in forced marches and train transports to camps located further away from the front. Due to its position deep in Reich territory, the Dachau concentration camp was initially a collection point for prisoners arriving from the concentration camps of Auschwitz, Natzweiler, Flossenbürg, and Buchenwald. Scores of prisoners perished during the rail transports and marches. The order to evacuate the Dachau concentration camp and its subcamps was issued only a few days before the arrival of American troops. The abandoning of the subcamps of the Kaufering complex began on April 23 1945. Three days later the first marching columns left the main Dachau camp, heading southward. The SS forcibly evacuated on transports or mercilessly herded along on forced marches at least 25,000 prisoners from the Dachau camp system.

During these marches, also called the "death marches", at least one thousand prisoners died. They died of disease, undernourishment, and exhaustion. If a prisoner collapsed or, fully exhausted, simply could not continue, they were

Prisoners from the Kaufering subcamp on a "death march" in Landsberg am Lech, April 1945

Women prisoners from the Dachau concentration camp on a "death march" in Percha, Lake Starnberg, April 28 1945

"[...] we could see the furtive parting of curtains as German civilians peered out at us. To our surprise a few of them came out and tried to offer us some bread, but the result was disastrous. Hundreds of starving inmates would descend on the benefactor, often knocking him or her down. The bread was immediately torn to pieces, and the guards set upon the mob. Each time this happened several more bodies were left by the side of the road."

Contemporary witness account of a death march;
Solly Ganor, prisoner in the Dachau concentration camp 1944–1945

beaten or shot to death by SS guards. The route of the marches passed through numerous villages and small towns. Scores of residents witnessed the brutal marches. Since 1989 municipalities along the routes of the "death marches" have erected 22 identical "death march monuments" by the sculptor Hubertus von Pilgrim. At the intersection of Theodor-Heuss-Straße / Sudetenlandstraße in Dachau, a "death march monument" was erected in 2001 in remembrance of the ordeal and suffering of the victims.

VISITOR INFORMATION

Contact
General information
Telephone: + 49 (0) 8131/ 66 99 70 (Monday–Friday 9 a.m.– 5 p.m.)
Fax: + 49 (0) 8131/ 22 35
Email: info@kz-gedenkstaette-dachau.de
Homepage: www.kz-gedenkstaette-dachau.de

Postal address administration, library, and archive
Alte Römerstraße 75, 85221 Dachau

Address Visitors' Center
Pater-Roth-Straße 2a, 85221 Dachau

Opening times / Admission
Daily 9 a.m.– 5 p.m.
Closed on December 24.
Admission is free. No prior registration or booking is necessary.

Archive and Library use
Tuesday–Friday 9 a.m.– 5 p.m.
Prior registration required:
archiv@kz-gedenkstaette-dachau.de or
bibliothek@kz-gedenkstaette-dachau.de

For general research inquiries:
wissenschaft@kz-gedenkstaette-dachau.de

Booking of tours and seminars
Only through the booking form on the Memorial Site's website:
www.kz-gedenkstaette-dachau.de

ACKNOWLEDGEMENTS

Dachau Concentration Camp Memorial Site. A Tour

Published for the Dachau Concentration Camp Memorial Site by Dr. Gabriele Hammermann and Dr. Stefanie Pilzweger-Steiner

Texts: Dr. Stefanie Pilzweger-Steiner along with Dr. Gabriele Hammermann, Waltraud Burger, Prof. Dr. Ludwig Eiber, Albert Knoll, and Michael Störk

Research and editing: Dr. Stefanie Pilzweger-Steiner

Proofreading: Boris Heczko, Berlin and Nancy Drechsler, Chemnitz
Translation: Paul Bowman, Grafing
Graphic design: Geraldine Braunsteffer, design wirkt, Munich

ISBN: 978-3-8316-4664-7

PHOTO CREDITS

akg-images GmbH, Berlin (photo Benno Gartner): p. 85 (r.); ap/dpa/picture alliance/Süddeutsche Zeitung Photo: p. 36 (u. l.), p. 83 (r.); Archiv Karmel Dachau: p. 67 (l.); Bielmeier Heinz, Dachau: p. 75 (u. r.); Bundesarchiv: p. 7, p. 8 (l.+r.), p. 9, p. 12 (l.), p. 36 (b. l.); Bundesarchiv (photo Friedrich Franz Bauer): p. 36 (u. r.+b. r.), p. 43 (b. l.+b.r.), p. 52 (r.); Büro für Gestaltung Wangler & Abele, Munich: front flap cover, p. 29; Cipollaro Costanza Luisa, Vienna: p. 46 (b. r.); dpa: p. 69 (b.); Eckstein Richard, Amorbach: p. 46 (b. l.); Fackelmann Michael, Munich: p. 19 (c.+b.); Freund William M., Durban: p. 40; Grevet Johanna, Vienna: p. 46 (u.); Hofer Monika u. Dümmler Ulrike, Munich: p. 48 (l.), p. 61 (r.); ITS Bad Arolsen: p. 49 (b.); Jørgensen Niels, Dachau: p. 70 (r.); Keystone: p. 68 (b.); KZ-Gedenkstätte Dachau: p. 12 (r.), p. 23, p. 30 (b.), p. 35 (u.+b.), p. 39, p. 43 (u.), p. 48 (r.), p. 49 (u.), p. 51 (l.+r.), p. 55 (l.+r.), p. 57 (u. l.+u. r.+b. l.), p. 61 (l.), p. 64 (l.+r.), p. 65 (u.+b.), p. 72 (l.), p. 75 (u. l.+b.), p. 80 (r.), p. 83 (l.); Landesamt für Digitalisierung, Breitband und Vermessung Bayern, Munich: p. 27; Luftbilddatenbank Dr. Carls, Würzburg: p. 24; Luftbildverlag Bertram, Memmingerberg: p. 66 (r.); Musienko Jurij, Kiev: p. 45 (l.); Stefan Müller-Naumann, Architekturfotografie, Munich: cover, back page, p. 22, p. 30 (u.), p. 33–34, p. 37–38, p. 41–42, p. 44, p. 47, p. 50, p. 53–54, p. 59–60, p. 62 (l.), p. 63, p. 66 (l.), p. 67 (r.), p. 68 (u.), p. 69 (u.), p. 70 (l.), p. 73–74, p. 77 (r.), p. 78, p. 81–82, p. 84, p. 86 Państwowy Instytut Naukowy – Instytut Śląski, Oppeln: p. 57 (b. r.); Rosemann Simone, Ebbs: p. 45 (c.); Scherl / Süddeutsche Zeitung Photo: p. 5; Staatsarchiv Würzburg: p. 32; Stadtarchiv Dachau: p. 79 (u.+b.); Stadtarchiv Landsberg am Lech: p. 85 (l.); Stadtarchiv München (photo Wilhelm Weiler): p. 6; Stanjek Klaus, Potsdam (photo Carl Linke): p. 45 (r.); Stiftung Brandenburgische Gedenkstätten, Gedenkstätte und Museum Sachsenhausen: p. 72 (r.); Süddeutsche Zeitung Photo (photo Alfred Haase): p. 20; UPI / Süddeutsche Zeitung Photo: p. 62 (r.); USHMM, Washington D.C.: p. 14 (u.+c.+b.), p. 16–17, p. 19 (u.), p. 52 (l.), p. 56, p. 58 (l.+r.), p. 77 (l.), p. 80 (l.); Yad Vashem: p. 31.

With the generous support of:

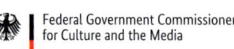 Federal Government Commissioner for Culture and the Media

 Bavarian State Ministry of Education and Cultural Affairs, Sciences and the Arts